JACK MAPANJE was born of Yao and Ny~~~
Kadango Village, Mangochi Di~~ ~
went to school at Kadang~
Catholic Secondary School
diploma in Education from
M.Phil degree from the Uni
joined the staff of the Depar
College, University of Malaw   ..∪⌐king as
a research student in linguisti   ..⌐ɪty College, London
in the early 1980s.

Of Chameleons and Gods received the Rotterdam
International Poetry Award in 1988. Mapanje was arrested
soon after this book was banned in Malawi. He was
imprisoned in Malawi and detained without Charge or Trial
from September 1987 to May 1991. His second volume of
Poetry, *The Chattering Wagtails of Mikuyu Prison*, written
while he was detained, was published by Heinemann in 1993.

JACK MAPANJE

OF CHAMELEONS AND GODS

POEMS

Sylvia + Brian

with love

Jack Mapanje

19/9/88

HEINEMANN

Heinemann Educational Publishers
A division of Heinemann Publishers (Oxford) Ltd
Halley Court, Jordan Hill, Oxford OX2 8EJ

Heinemann: A Division of Reed Publishing (USA) Inc.
361 Hanover Street, Portsmouth, NH 03801-3912, USA

Heinemann Educational Books (Nigeria) Ltd
PMB 5205, Ibadan
Heinemann Educational Boleswa
PO Box 10103, Village Post Office, Gaborone, Botswana

FLORENCE PRAGUE PARIS MADRID
ATHENS MELBOURNE JOHANNESBURG
AUCKLAND SINGAPORE TOKYO
CHICAGO SAO PAULO

British Library Cataloguing in Publication Data

A catalogue record or this book is available from the British Library

ISBN 0435 91194 5

Printed and bound in Great Britain by
Cox & Wyman Ltd, Reading, Berkshire

94 95 96 10 9 8 7 6 5 4 3 2

Contents

Introduction

The verse in this volume spans some ten turbulent years in which I have been attempting to find a voice or voices as a way of preserving some sanity. Obviously where personal voices are too easily muffled, this is a difficult task; one is tempted like the chameleon, who failed to deliver Chiuta's message of life, to bask in one's brilliant camouflage. But the exercise has been, if nothing else, therapeutic; and that's no mean word in our circumstances!

Jack Mapanje
Zomba 1981

Of Chameleons and Gods

Kabula Curio-Shop

Black wood between carefully bowed legs
  the eyes red over bellows and smoke
  the sharpening of axes, adzes, carvers
  the chopping, the whittling and such
  carving such scooping and scooping
  then the sandpapering and smoothing

Black wood between carefully bowed legs
  such energy release and the price
  bargained away, would you imagine
  now a broken symbol thrown careless
  in the nook of a curio-shop: a lioness
  broken legs, broken neck, broken udder?

Song of Chickens

Master, you talked with bows,
Arrows and catapults once
Your hands steaming with hawk blood
To protect your chicken.

Why do you talk with knives now,
Your hands teaming with eggshells
And hot blood from your own chicken?
Is it to impress your visitors?

A Marching Litany to
Our Martyrs
(3 March 1971)

In the name of our dear brothers dead
Are we really marching to these tin-drums
Rattling the skeleton beat of heroic
Bones long laid asleep?

The planes that dropped white emergency papers

Do we really halt to revere perplexed
Elders now only shades shaking and
Tossing synthetic calabashes of chibuku
Beer which numbs their brain?

Those stooges' cars and houses fire-gutted

Have we really about swung to these
Frantic maxi-skirts slit to thighs
Opening to whispers and caresses of
Midnight breezes and coins?

And the barricades and bridges shattered

Do we now salute the squealing laughters
Of the broken hearts in their shells
Clicking their crumpled tin-cans of
Goat-urine to their bungled dreams?

What of the tear-gas and the bullets on their heads?

Do we now troop past the skeletal mothers
Before their sons' burial mounds weeping
With broken bowls of rotten weevils
And shards of sour brew for their libation?

And those bitter tears and the blood that gushed

In the name of our growing bellies,
Batons, buggers and bastards rife,
Let us revel in parades, lowering the emblem
Of the precious bones long laid asleep.

Amen!

If Chiuta Were Man*

I   The Soft Landing

Woman, hold my shoulders
We'll drift and drift until
We reach the promised Nsinja
Forest and river of life.

When our safari is done
We'll tell all animals and
Chiuta of our soft landing
Imploring them to follow suit.

Meanwhile hold on woman
Let's glide and glide
On our pioneer project:
Hope is our only hope.

*These four pieces are based on a Malawian creation myth that
pervades oral traditions.

II   The First Fire

Hard wood upon soft wood twirling
Sparks a sudden riot of mothers and babies.

Corrosive flames devour Nsinja Forest
Chiuta's abode belches and blazes.

When frenzied lions storm, jackals
Crackle gaping at man's invention.

The stampede thus whacked thuds away
Free from the hissing eggshells.

Only dogs, tails between legs
Cower under the Man's fiery arm.

III   Man On Chiuta's Ascension

When you disgruntled spiralled
On spider's frail thread
Swearing you'd see us die feeling
The pain of our own invention,

When you thundering angry voices
That still send us scurrying for
Shelter promised your urine to save us
From our unquenchable fire,

When you on your multi-coloured
Bow on Ntiwa Hill declared
You'd stop your bleeding urine
If we did not improve,

Why, Chiuta, scampering on
Spider's thread to your Ivory Tower,
Why didn't you also warn
Our eyes would forever be smokey?

IV   So God Became a Chameleon

A muezzin
with gelded
tongue
slunk in
celibacy

A politician
empiric
muffing
easy balls
fearing fear

The Tussle

And so Son
next time you're
on sand playing animal
play not hyena carried
away by lion rather
the lion,
if forced
carry him away
make the hyena that
killed the lion,
when he grumbles
tell him it's only
a game – animal game
you are men and
he'll lead the next
chick-stealing
pig-blood-tapping
party anyway.
You've seen the latest
tussle!

The New Platform Dances

Haven't I danced the big dance
Compelled the rains so dust could
Soar high above like when animals
Stampede? Haven't I in animal
Skins wriggled with amulets
Rattled with anklets
Scattered nervous women
With snakes around my neck
With spears in these hands
Then enticed them back
With flywhisk's magic?
Haven't I moved with all
Concentric in the arena
To the mystic drums
Dancing the half-nude
Lomwe dance
Haven't I?

Haven't my wives at mortars sang
Me songs of praise, of glory,
How I quaked the earth
How my skin trembled
How my neck peaked
Above all dancers
How my voice throbbed
Like the father-drum
I danced to
Haven't they?

12

Now, when I see my daughters writhe
Under cheating abstract
Voices of slack drums, ululate
To babble-idea-men-masks
Without amulets or anklets,
Why don't I stand up
To show them how we danced
Chopa, how IT was born?
Why do I sit still
Why does my speech choke
Like I have not danced
Before? Haven't I
Danced the bigger dance?
Haven't I?

Messages

1

Tell her we still expose our bottoms
Eat unseasoned *nsima* with *bonongwe*
From a wooden ladle our hands unscented,
We still sleep in slums rolling
In bird-droppings, friends of fleas,
Maggots. Tell her our pleasure
Is still in the pattering tin-drums
That convoke these tatters in the cold
Of dawn to quench hangovers. Tell
Her besides, a cat sees best at night
Not much at noon and so when time
Comes, while she eats and drinks
While she twists and shouts, rides
And travels, we shall refuse
To reach her our stuff of fortune
Even if she called us witches!
We swear by our fathers dead!

2

The red neon light illuminates
Her loose butterfly skirt
The iron rippled hair
Her pink veneer smile

Her moist hand grips mine
Her forefinger goring my palm
What . . . ? She . . . ? – nail varnish
On my palm . . . 'a beer please . . . '

Her back swirls off me
Gassed by reeking perfumes, sitting:
Tattering curtains, doors to bathrooms
Couples in corners unabashed

She comes back thick-lip-cigaretted
The chest jutting into the world generously
The lashes greased bluer
'Come from far . . . ? Tired . . . eh . . . ?'

I reply a struck-Portugese-match laughter
As I try to whisper her navel name
'Asawilunda, your mother at Kadango greets you and . . . '
Oh, already floating to the next customer?

3

Did you think it was a hunting party
Where after a fall from chasing a hare
You laughed together an enemy shaking
Dust off your bottom, a friend reaching
You your bow and arrow? Or a game safari
Where you patted your hounds before
The halloo? Did you think this the bush
Where the party would take the best of
Their kill to the Chief so he could allow
Them more hunting bush next time? No,
Mother, it's a war here, a lonely war
Where you hack your own way single-handed
To make anything up to the Shaka of
The tribe! It's fine the earth's fertile!

The Glorious Past

Those women with tattoos on their navels
beads around their waists and *zipini*
on their noses, those women on leopard
skins surrounded by greased gourds
snuff on their palms and sneezing their
brilliant past to whoever they could
honour or gurgling their past mysteries
from their bedecked hookahs –

                              Can they be

These women in plastic bangles
coughing in broken proverbs
rejoicing their son is back
the village is blessed and appealing
in the name of our politeness why can't
I toss another calabash of *masese* beer
before we together unravel
the story of their precious glorious past?

Requiem to a Fallen Son

I still remember the songs
The happy songs by the chaperons
Of our village in the middle of the night:
The child is born Gods bless him
The child is here Spirits spare him
The child is male Witches protect him
And the ululations confirmed
A sure-footed birth
As the village blazed in bonfires
Dustbin drums carelessly talking
'How the mother giggled digging up
The Child from an anthill!'
Mother told us at the fireside
And if there was blood
In the breaking of the cord
They must have made sure to hide it
For I saw, I felt, I smelt nothing
But the happiness of men and women
Reeling to taut drums
Roaring in jubilation of your birth, Son.

Before Chilembwe Tree

1

Didn't you say we should trace
your footprints unmindful of
quagmires, thickets and rivers
until we reached your *nsolo* tree?

Now, here I seat my gourd of beer
on my little fire throw my millet
flour and my smoked meat while
I await the second coming.

2

Why does your mind boggle:
Who will offer another gourd
Who will force another step
To hide our shame?

The goat blood on the rocks
The smoke that issued
The drums you danced to
And the rains hoped for—

You've chanted yourselves hoarse
Chilembwe is gone in your dust
Stop lingering then:
Who will start another fire?

Dope

land
    scapes
        whirl
      daze
   and
halt
  lens
    focus
       pools
    around
  tree
   stumps
      where
women
   sit
     inhaling
       dagga
         profuse

```
            men
  clutching
            fishing
                    rods
            but
  catching
                    tad
                            poles
            sulking
                        and
        rotating
                            crystal –
                            lization
                            negatives
                            through
                            bromide
```

The Cheerful Girls at Smiller's Bar, 1971

The prostitutes at Smiller's Bar beside the dusty road
Were only girls once in tremulous mini-skirts and oriental
Beads, cheerfully swigging Carlsbergs and bouncing to
Rusty simanje-manje and rumba booming in the juke-box.
They were striking virgins bored by our Presbyterian
Prudes until a true Presbyterian came one night. And like
To us all the girls offered him a seat on cheap planks
In the dark backyard room choked with diesel-oil clouds
From a tin-can lamp. Touched the official rolled his eyes
To one in style. She said no. Most girls only wanted
A husband to hook or the fruits of Independence to taste
But since then mini-skirts were banned and the girls
Of Smiller's Bar became 'ugly prostitutes to boot!'

Today the girls still giggle about what came through
The megaphones: the preservation of our traditional
et cetera . . .

The Sweet Brew at Chitakale

The old woman squats before a clay jar of *thobwa*
She uncovers the basket lid from the jar and
Stirs attention with a gourdful of the brew.

The customers have all been here: cyclists
In dripping sweat have deposited their coins
In the basket gulping down their share,

Pedestrians on various chores have talked
Before the exchange and then cooled their
Parched throats to their money's worth,

But this bus passenger bellows for a gourdful
From the window, drinks deliberately slowly until
The conductor presses the go-button –

The woman picks up the pieces of her broken
Gourd, and dusting her bottom, again squats
Confronting her brew with a borrowed cup.

The Palm Trees at Chigawe

You stood like women in green
Proud travellers in panama hats and java print
Your fruit-milk caused monkeys and shepherds to scramble
Your dry leaves were banners for night fishermen
But now stunted trees stand still beheaded –
A curious sight for the tourists

These Too Are Our Elders

Watch these elders. They always come at night
In bloated plumage, tossing you on their
Avocado noses, inhaling all the free air out
Of you. Their masks carry fatal viruses.

One came the other night draped in hyena skins
His face showing amid the fluffed out ostrich
Feathers, twisting his sinews in a frenzied
Dance. At work I was unseating him, he preached.

But I too went to the village he had visited.
They said I should ask him next time why
He always came at night, why he pretended
I was more useful than the Whiteman once in

My seat, and why he sent me to school at all?
Well, he merely backslid through the bamboo rafters
Showering behind rotten amulets and mice shit!
Why do these elders always exploit our disbelief?

On African Writing (1971)

You've rocked at many passage rites, at drums
Mothers clapping their admiration of your
Initiation voices – now praises of decay
That still mesmerize some; at times you've
Yodled like you'd never become men gallant
Hunting, marrying, hating, killing. But
In your masks you've sung on one praise
After another. You have sung mouth-songs!
Men struggling to justify what you touched
Only, heard merely! Empty men! Do you realise
You are still singing initiation tunes?
You have not chimed hunting-marrying –
Fighting-killing praises until you've
Stopped all this nonsense about drinking
Palm wine from plastic tumblers!
And these doggerels, these sexual-tribal
Anthropological-political doggerels!
Don't you think even mothers will stop
Quaking some day? Don't you realise
Mothers also ache to see their grand
Children at home playing *bau* on sofas?
Why do you always suppose mothers
Never want to see you at these conferences
They are for ever hearing about?

Why do you imagine they never understand
Things? They too can be alert to all this
Absurdity about what you think they think!
You've sung many songs, some superb
But these lip-songs are most despicable!

Sketches from London

Handshakes and Best Wishes

Late. The heat of September afternoons
Pours hardening your face, cracking your lips
Airport hustle, hubbub, bags and bag slips
In the balcony above the disciples toss
To expected final handshakes and best wishes
But their zealous hands must falter as a rush
Hand nervously alarms towards the runway
Sentence: Oh, well . . drink from the source!

In truth there had been enough handshakes
The village neighbour cursing his son for
'Getting out through the school window, shaming me!'
The Chief with a bubbling calabash hoping
His best wishes brought back everflowing calabashes
The girl-cousin declaring another marriage postponed –
'A rabbit must have run between your legs, you!'
And mother's dry twig pecking at the sere earth, quiet.

The handshakes and best wishes were many and
As we are spared more today: the choking gossip
And the extravagant pomp and speeches; even
The captain's beaten apology for the delay at
Entebe as Idi Amin issues the pass, releases.

Sketches of London

The source: flaming cardboard boxes with squeaking
Staircases. Like smoked cockroaches we sneak out
Of peeling caches; the conduits bleak behind plate-
Glass; the concrete blocks grey, unmoved – the brush
Won't do. Plastic litterbags burst open drip in mews
Poodles' muck on pavements, the ladies don't mind
Refuse collectors went on strike weeks and weeks ago
Glory be! Whoever said there was a fountain here?

The Serpentine: lovely recreation; but if they had
Mosquitoes here this city would be a desert. Thames
Banks: they picked up a dead woman the other day
Her lungs were found wrapped up in World War soot
She must have been living here thirty years, they said.
The Tower: King Henry's abattoirs. His wives' regalia
Still trail amid the steaming guillotines
The bath tubs are meticulously kept for ten pence.

I knew a playful priest once back home
I was always late for his catechism lessons
He gave me three strokes to show me the way
He said, but the cane snapped before the fourth
In anger he threw away the broken pieces
And instead touched the little thing between
My legs. Didn't I giggle, running away!

Drinking the Water from its Source

Distancing ourselves now our metaphors sharpen
We say drink the water from its source naïvely
Probably thinking of its purity, our salvation
Or the dead empire. We know only too well that
All water springs from sources so inscrutible
Yet drinking water far from the sources we often
Exalt our images heedless of the minor details:
Streams gather debris from antique sun-spots
Depositing the silt onto infinite sand-beds
The gliding Shire River mystifies us watering
Our golden lives, and tantalized we then conclude
The source of the waters must be more exotic.

But drinking the water from the source is like
A prayer: after we have slipped out of our
Sandals washing our grey feet for the moment
We only seek the point of our troubled voices
Hoping thereby to reassemble our broken confidence
We know that after the prayer we'll slip back
Into our sandals buckling more dust, probing
Greater salvation, again watching the hour when
The muezzin should raise his voice for another
Congregation. Drinking water from the sources
We must turn back to the peripheral mosaics of home
Revealing the depth of their natural negatives.

The First Train to Liverpool

(A letter for Angela)

No last minute haggling about prices
Of curry-chicken first at Balaka
No stinking Afro-wigs into your mouths
No leaping from bags of peanuts into
Baskets of tomato, cheerfully quarrelling
Nor finally sitting on half a buttock
Euston station contacts and dialogues
Through wires and innumerable papers
Only comfort welcomes aboard a sudden silence
That soon reigns, our eyes weighing and
Quickly avoiding each other between
The beverages and the local papers.

Runcorn station welcomes aboard a haunting
Quiet where men obviously build more paper
Walls against other men. No curios, no mats
No herbs sell through windows. No mothers
Suckle their crying babies. No jokes about
The rains held up by your charms this year!
At Lime Street itself, not even a drunk staggers
Out perhaps announcing his newly acquired
Cornerstones. Only recorded voices bid you
Come again before the engulfing impenetrable
Crowds. But the maddening quiet soon recedes
Locating a bright tarnished face once known.

Travelling in London Tubes

(for VSOs, 1973 Childs Hall, Reading)

There is something funny about
the dust back home
the way it blows
naïvely with the wind
and carelessly settles
on flowers and maize gardens
blemishing the green
the way it rolls
behind the big cars on the dusty roads
like cotton wool ashed
leaving you rubbing your eyes
like a child,
Yet you can avoid it all so easily too
just keep your head up, above,
or even laugh
and let the big cars pass.

But here, even the dust is subtle
the way it blows
with the seemingly fresh breeze
and settles
on your window-sill
in your eyes
and nose,
even the dust is subtle here;

And it is not until the day is out
if you should stand at your window
facing the breeze apparently blowing cool
it is not until your sudden
aitchoo!
that you begin to see how much
charcoal was in your nose
eyes
lungs
travelling in those lovely tubes.

From Florrie Abraham Witness, December 1972

There are times when their faith in gods
Really fascinates me. Take when the Anglican
Priest with all pomp and ceremony married
Abraham and Florrie, why didn't he realise
Abe and Florrie would eventually witness
The true Jehovah in his most pristine? And silly
Little Florrie, couldn't she foresee the run against
The only cards possible when she said her
'Yes, I do; for kids or for none?' And when
Florrie's mother dear, with all her Anglican
Limping love for her first and only daughter
Still intact, even when she thought she might
Still visit the prodigals notwithstanding, how
Couldn't she see that she too would be booted out
Landing carelessly bruised and in *Moça-
mbique*! The buggers! They surely deserve it;
They deserve such a good kick on their bottom.
I mean, there are times when their faith just
Fails me. Take today, when silly little Florrie
Should scribble a funny epistle on stupid roll —
And Love did you have to call it thus? I mean,
It sounds so strangely imprudent of . . . But. . .
Anyway: Darling Brother, only God of Abraham
Knows how we escaped the petrol and matches
Yet we are all in good hands. They give us
Free flour, beans free and their kind of salted

Meat and fish. We've even built a ten-by-ten yard
Little hospital for our dear selves. Only we
Haven't got any soap. But we'll manage and do not
Be anxious over us here dear Brother; Mummie
And the kids are all in good shape. They send
Their Christmas greetings. Read well and, oh, note:
Psalms! Where in London is the blooming Bible?

Re-entering Chingwe's Hole

As the West End Allegro Subsides Today

(for Lan)

When you went on about those Trinidadian
Steel Bands and calypso in your Chichiri flat
I did not really care, I nodded only
Out of goodwill nor did I expect
The winds to blow us into another flat
On Chepstow Road and one London summer
Afternoon watch the whole carnival
Colourful, brisk, gently flowing towards
Notting Hill Gate graced by tuneful
Steel Bands as baby Martin watching cricket
On TV pulled out the plugs fidgeting
About being left alone to learn to crawl.
But as the West End allegro subsides today
And the periodic blurt of Zomba muezzins
Carelessly mingles with the crows of Chirunga
Estates to consummate our re-entry into
An otherwise cautious quiet green, tempers
Often fray. Shouldn't I have cared at all?

Visiting Zomba Plateau

Could I have come back to you to wince
Under the blur of your negatives,
To sit before braziers without the glow
Of charcoal, to cringe at your rivers
That without their hippos and crocs
Merely trickle gratingly down, to watch
Dragonflies that no longer fascinate and
Puff-adders that have lost their puff?
Where is your charming hyena tail—
Praying-mantis who cared for prayers once?
Where is the spirit that touched the hearts
Lightly – chameleon colours of home?
Where is your creation myth? Have I come
To witness the carving and jingling only of
Your bloated images and piddling mirrors?

Re-entering the Shrines of Zomba

At the gates the guardians have set up cockroaches and
Leeches to protect the shrines from stray iconoclasts

The tax-collectors ominously wink at each other
Weighing the genuineness of your travellers cheques

The secretaries tittilate freely about their bastards
Watching your first syllables. The Gods have deserted

These noble shrines. A new religion is born. And when
The sacrificial hour arrives, the custodians first

Surrender to the deception of demijohns, then gyrating
To rhythms of mystic drums, they shovel their satchels

Of neuroses onto the sacred rocks and bow. They seek no
Advice how to bring back willing dear old Gods; so the rains

Won't come; the rueful lambs refuse to bleat at the altars
And in the grottos benumbed virgins put out the candles.

Glory Be to Chingwe's Hole

Chingwe's Hole, you devoured the Chief's prisoners
Once, easy villagers decked in leopard colours
Pounding down their energies and their sight.
You choked minstrel lovers with wild granadilla
Once, rolling under burning flamboyant trees.

Do you remember Frog the carver carving Ebony Beauty?
Do you remember Frog's pin on Ebony Beauty's head
That brought Ebony to life? And when the Chief
Heard of a beauty betrothed to Frog, whose dogs
Beat up the bushes to claim Ebony for the Chief?

Even when Fly alarmed Frog of the impending hounds
Who cracked Fly's bones? Chingwe's Hole, woodpeckers
Once poised for vermillion strawberries merely
Watched fellow squirrels bundled up in sacks
Alive as your jaws gnawed at their brittle bones.

Chingwe's Hole, how dare I praise you knowing whose
Marrow still flows in murky Namitembo River below you?
You strangled our details boasting your plush dishes,
Dare I glorify your rope and depth epitomizing horror?

Standing on Bunda Hill

When her turtle scales peel
even the Chiefs must look away
lest the gods detain the rains
– they all fear here

Her mythical ears where Ngonis
choked fleeing Chewas once
reek of the teething days
of urchins smoking mice

Only the artist's version perhaps
a Berlings Kaunda bloodshot
mother Bunda in concrete, grunting
within the walls of her own muck –

Captures the view.

Epitaph for a Mad Friend

Do you remember in Mtendere buses
Stopping at Ulongwe to replenish
Through bus windows to poke curry-fried chicken
In urchin basins below, chewing, content,
Joking about the man who ties the rains each year?

Do you remember my mad friend standing
Suddenly there, paw-paw juice streaking down
His front from yester crop, and then
The tatters mockingly imploring:
*Andwanje suwa siwili, ambe likobili!**

Don't you remember the passengers roaring
With laughter and tears, and you turning to me:
'How dare I hit him on *his* head for my penny?'
And brushing, cruising on in hiccups down
The dusty road to the lake?

But on the eve of our eleventh Independence
Today after the beautiful tarmac to the lake
And my brief spell abroad,
I hear Mercy warn:
'Even Andwanje-suwa-siwili is gone!'

* *Hit me twice on my head and give me a penny for it.*

Gerrie's Season of Goodwill, 1975

(for Lan, Jim & Robin)

When Gerrie flew in to teach early this year
We introduced him to the lower house of the club
But the pub's effigy, papier-mâché Queen Victoria
Bemused him immensely. How could she still
Have the nerve to preside over the raffle of silver
Trophies, expats, bar-tenders, the few mortals—
the stalwart mess? He asked. Everyone was startled
By Gerrie's naïvety and his daring admission that
He'd never played golf in his life, that the expats
Silly gossip or their free exchange of tennis or
Bridge partners for life or the locals' gloating
Over their undeclared polygamies, bored him stiff.
But before we could allow Gerrie more enthusiastic
Words: that he'd come for a bit of the local culture
Really or for bottle walking! which was dangerous as he'd
Already gathered from the usually reliable rumours,
Sapato, our local authority on Gerrie's kind butted in
With, 'Just the sort for this year's squash trophy!'
Ordering of course, the fourth round of drinks. Well,
You can imagine what happens after such a start:
Round after round after pub after boiled eggs after
Laughter until Gerrie of course, summoned up enough
Courage to go it alone. Well, yesterday, didn't we have

47

To see Gerrie off, briefly? And when his precious neighbours
Subtly declared, 'You shouldn't have been so naughty
Really, you know, breaking other peoples laws
Deserves imprisonment back home, you remember;' Gerrie's
Wife offered them the Victorian bamboo chair and
The kids' games they could not pack. And Gerrie
Himself joked carelessly, 'I was only here for the beer!'

The Hounds in Puddles

The hounds were out again last week
Scaring the children playing ball in puddles outside

One child had a very bad trip
The hounds nearly mauled him to death

Wasn't I nervous!

Last night a blue-bill sparrow strayed into
Our crowded living room

The light blinded her to roost
The children laughing almost crushed her to death

Didn't my blood well!

It's been like this these sensitive years, you see,
With bits of smoke issuing under *nsolo* trees

But soon, I know,

The green hounds will maul these tender children
And the children the crispy sparrows

And I shudder.

For a Friend Taken, 1976

Even robots flick amber first
And you can whizz down the bloody
Road before the red if you like!

Waiting for the Electronic Forceps

(for Felix)

Michael, your prayer for the butterfly
clutched between your warm fingers once
that the Lord might still grant her
a distant sense of humour with the Sun
or the bright colours of her wings
despite the garbage breath of this earth,
your prayer was strained.

                And whoever took
Seriously drunken Presbyters or toothless
shepherds who fear to undertake their
precious sheep lost in cold abattoirs?
Not even the Sun itself now, I imagine,
when your handcuffed butterfly sprawls
in the freezing dark walls – waiting
for the electronic pins and forceps.

For David Kerr & Lavinia Spencer, December 1976

The moral of the plane tree in Talbot Square
How it braces the seasons and tells our time

Your cheerless grey sky matching the concrete walls

The Londoner's wink of the eye and tilt of the head
– Our type of communication

Your blues with the homebrew bitter at Purfleet
Reflecting demented Dracula house opposite

Even the publisher's patron tone on
Our verse at John and Gizzy's wine and cheese

Today these tenuous memories strangely tighten
                             And dear Lavinia,
Today I recall our Paddington tube station nerves
Of a bomb happily defused

And your Moscow souvenir cigars I left unkindly
In the black plastic litterbag outside the door

For as the golden Sun went down on us
Today another comrade went in

And did my heart jump!

The familiar landscapes and banal images of home
For whom the lips falsely part

Blur.

The House that Florrie Intended

She was building a stone house here once
To match with the times, she carelessly declared
Selecting her slabs and passing them on to
Her husband to lay the foundation. Young
Abu and Jemu playing corkfloat beachball
Rolled on the fine dry sands of Koko Bay
Edi and Lizi washing their cassava to dry
In the hot sun, caught little fish in their
Bamboo baskets screeching in joy and triumph
And on this tablet of rock I sat half-nude
I remember hatching a little revolution with
Myself, brooding on an arched life, my arms
Cupping the chin, the brow tensed, the legs
Crossed, watching the endless blue waters of
The vast lake curl, break, lap-lapping at my
Feet as little fish nibbled at my toes. Then
A loin-cloth fisherman, emerging from the men
Bent mending their broken nets under the shade
Of the lone beachtree, jumped into a canoe
Fettered to a nearby colony of reeds and grass
He sculled away lazily perhaps to check the night's
Fishtraps. Meanwhile, beyond those rocks that
Drill in birdshit like breasts in white bras
Or two eggshells, a sharp fisheagle lingering
Swooped down for his afternoon *chambo*. And
Florrie passed on the morning's last stone to
Abraham. What transpired after that, I cannot tell
Except that I dared briefly abroad and I gather

Florrie witnessed in protest; and I gather her
Radiogram, those rumba records the kids so much
Cherished, and the spring bed and matress, and
The fridge – the spoons and forks too witnessed her
Departure. And today when Florrie's kids stand
Desperate at my embarrassed door, I've come to see
The straggling cornerstones of her house intended.

In Memory of Matthew, 1976

You should have gone down with malaria
I'd have brought you those *nakatobwa* mangoes
You so much cherished,

We'd have joked about the mosquitoes
We once smoked to death with acacia leaves –
Chattering kids picking each other's lice,

I'd have told you about the squirrel
We caught stealing cabbage
In our backyard garden the other day;

And that pear-seedling
You took to transplant,
Why didn't you allow it to sprout?

You should have rested with folded arms
Calm on the chest,
Why did you have to shrink thus?

On His Royal Blindness
Paramount Chief Kwangala

I admire the quixotic display of your paramountcy
How you brandish our ancestral shields and spears
Among your warriors dazzled by your loftiness
But I fear the way you spend your golden breath
Those impromptu, long-winded tirades of your might
In the heat, do they suit your brittle constitution?

I know I too must sing to such royal happiness
And I am not arguing. Wasn't I too tucked away in my
Loin-cloth infested by jiggers and fleas before
Your bright eminence showed up? How could I quibble
Over your having changed all that? How dare I when
We have scribbled our praises all over our graves?

Why should I quarrel when I too have known mask
Dancers making troubled journeys to the gold mines
On bare feet and bringing back fake European gadgets
The broken pipes, torn coats, crumpled bowler hats,
Dangling mirrors and rusty tincans to make their
Mask dancing strange? Didn't my brothers die there?

No, your grace, I am no alarmist nor banterer
I am only a child surprised how you broadly disparage

Me shocked by the tedium of your continuous palaver. I
Adore your majesty. But paramountcy is like a raindrop
On a vast sea. Why should we wait for the children to
Tell us about our toothless gums or our showing flies?

Making Our Clowns Martyrs

(or Returning Home Without Chauffeurs)

We all know why you have come back home with no
National colours flanking your black mercedes benz.
The radio said the toilets in the banquet halls of
Your dream have grown green creepers and cockroaches
Which won't flush, and the orders you once shouted
To the concubines so mute have now locked you in.
Hard luck my friend. But we all know what currents
Have stroked your temper. You come from a breed of
Toxic frogs croaking beside the smoking marshes of
River Shire, and the first words you breathed were
Snapped by the lethal mosquitoes of this morass.
We knew you would wade your way through the arena
Though we wondered how you had got chosen for the benz.
You should have been born up the hills, brother where
Lake waters swirl and tempers deepen with each season
Of the rains. There you'd see how the leopards of
Dedza hills comb the land or hedge before their assault.
But welcome back to the broken reed-fences, brother;
Welcome home to the poached reed-huts you left behind;
Welcome to these stunted pit-latrines where only
The pungent whiff of buzzing green flies gives way.
You will find your idle ducks still shuffle and fart
In large amounts. The black dog you left still sniffs

Distant recognition, lying, licking its leg-wounds. And
Should the relatives greet you with nervous curiosity
In the manner of masks carved in somebody's image,
There is always across the dusty road, your mad auntie.
She alone still thinks this new world is going shit.
She alone still cracks about why where whys are crimes.

When This Carnival Finally Closes

When this frothful carnival finally closes, brother
When your drumming veins dry, these very officers
Will burn the scripts of the praises we sang to you
And shatter the calabashes you drank from. Your
Charms, these drums, and the effigies blazing will
Become the accomplices to your lie-achieved world!
Your bamboo hut on the beach they'll make a bonfire
Under the cover of giving their hero a true traditional
Burial, though in truth to rid themselves of another
Deadly spirit that might otherwise have haunted them,
And at the wake new mask dancers will quickly leap
Into the arena dancing to tighter skins, boasting
Other clans of calabashes as the undertakers jest:
What did he think he would become, a God? The devil!

Assembling Another Voice

Steve Biko is Dead

The Boers have poked another
Human's sparkling eyes
With electric tongs
Soldering his sharp brain to metal

Steve Biko is dead
The most liberal of Western
Papers will probably
Report his death thus:

'The duffers have wafted
Biko with another poisonous wand
Of a gorgeous apartheid peacock
Ogling sanity into slumber...'

That Biko was another Man
With a wife, a child, a conscience
And the right to live ordinarily
Fighting in peace,

Of the restive ship behind,
Why or for how long
Steve Bikos will waste
We'll not bother to ask.

Who dares to budge
These precious days
And give evidence
For hope bereft?

Messages from Soweto

(Go back to develop your own homeland!)

Today they have set up mirrors
that reflect their ageing arrogance
adopting a stern detrimental line –
They alone know what to think.

In the darkrooms of our universe
negatives assume the power of their original
images, naïve termites are unleashed
To diet on the meagre corner-poles of our globe.

Exampli gratia, the other week:
colourful tadpoles hop about
the fringes of our dim pavements
In the sometimes cool rains –

Didn't they become subversive
metaphors confusing the Michelin tyres
that crushed them! Even to pee,
Which youth does not need clearance?

After Wiriyamu Village Massacre
by Portuguese

No, go back into your exile, go back quick.
When those Portuguese soldiers abducted
Falencha's baby quietly strapped on her back
And scattered its precious brain on Falencha's
Own maize grinding stone, when those soldiers
Grabbed and hacked Dinyero's only son
With Dinyero herself stubbornly watching
Or when they burnt down Faranando in his own
Hut as he tried to save Alefa his senile wife—
Where, where was your hand? Tell me that!
And if you helped Adrian Hastings report
The Portuguese atrocities to humans, where,
Where is your verse? You have no shame!
No, go back until our anger has simmered.

An Elegy for Mangochi Fishermen

Today even those fireflies have become
The banners for our night fishermen
The crabs and *dondolos* dare not
Peep out of their crevices.

The virgin canoe we once boasted about
Holding the head or pushing the rear
Pulling the lips or rolling on poles,
The canoe has capsized, the carvers drowned.

Those loin-cloths dripping, the muscles
Twitching with power, the husky voices chanting
About the delicious chambo dishes expected
Even the toes we once crushed dragging
Our canoe from the arid Namizimu mountains
To the soft beaches of this golden lake –

We will not cast in tender herbs to cure.
Today, you gone, the vigil wax has melted away
The light is out in our cryptic recesses
We must all lie in pitch dark stakes.

Should we then wipe our sticky brows
In the heat of another October? Should we fell
More poles to roll another canoe to the beach?
Is it worth it assembling another voice?

We Wondered About the Mellow Peaches

So, behind the heavy backyard orchard
And your generous invitations Alberto
To guava tart today and mango pudding tomorrow
Behind the spate of those Chilobwe township
Lambs brutally chopped in their dark huts
Where even undertakers dare not tread,

                          There
Were whiskers, Alberto, to map the moves
And pay the bills? Why, why did I waste my
Melodious song excoriating parochial squirrels
And hammerheads for readily running messages
Up and down bowing peachtrees and bringing
Flashy girls with mellow peaches and vermilion
Strawberries into lascivious range-rovers?
I should have erected them an edifice instead
I should have set up votive slabs from Mphunzi
Hills, chalked the rude walls with gentle
Gazelles and the lore about sweet foundlings –
To while away my temper. And yet, how could
The chameleon have lost grip of his own colours?
And did we need the restive decade to uncover
The plot? And this fuss about conspiracies and goats,
Didn't we all wonder about the mellow peaches?

April 1978, the Prisoners Quietly Back

For goodness sake Sweetie, let's stop fretting
About turbid top cockroaches without the brains
To penetrate even their own images. Let us
For once when the prisoners are quietly home
Enjoy the fruits of the evergreen landscape of
Zomba plateau. Let us walk up this Colossus
When the winding avenues are littered with
The purple of jacarandas and the tongues of
Flames-of-the-forests.
                              At the sawmill let us
Pause to greet plateau boys buying their fresh
Luscious granadilla and gorgeous strawberries
And up Mlungusi fountain let us select a rock
To sit down on and as the sparrows hop about
The tree branches twittering, let us chew our
Chambo sandwiches to the welling crests splattering
Nervously down the river. Or let us fondle our
Released hope hurtling down the turf in a strange
Joy today when the prisoners are quietly back.

Nor Will I Believe the Glorious Retreat

(A letter: I thought you'd all crack up
after your endless et cetera, but obviously
you've. . .)

If you ask me Michael, today even Angela thought
She too might streak in the heat of our pointless
Monotonous ranting, so fuming about the et cetera
She run up Mlungusi river and on a prodigious rock
Collapsed sweltering under a purpling jacaranda
But deep-blue-purple flowers rained cool on her
Like pigeons at Trafalgar Square once, she boasted;
And as suddenly those squirrels and cockroaches
That gnawed at our precious nerves and private
Cabbages fossilized into a silly little joke,
And those beleaguered decades without a smile or
Shame retreated, leaving behind dewed Carlsbergs
And beaming *samusas* for the pick. But you know how I
Read time when she should take her stock so starkly
Naïvely; don't I still remember how cockroaches
And squirrels breed; how could I believe their
Retreat? But for once even Angela who never really
Talks, carelessly said: I think I'll go shit on
The road tomorrow and tell the retreat that I have
Sinned grossly. I'm sure Father Patrick will heartily
Ask me to count my beaded Carlsbergs by the tens!

At the Metro:
Old Irrelevant Images

(for Blaise)

They are still so anthropologically tall here
Still treating you in irrelevant tribal metaphors:
Somalis have softer skins, they drink milk; they say
(And yours is cracking, you drink *kachasu*!)

Even the most knowledgeable still slip back
Apologizing to you in banal Tarzan images:
The children still know mostly Tarzans at school; they say
(Tarzans choked me too in the fifties, damn it!)

But the College girls' sit-in about rapists was
A bit of a change, and Mrs Thatcher's et cetera
Against overseas students; and, the publisher's dinner!
(How are the jacarandas I left blooming, otherwise?)

On Being Asked to Write
a Poem for 1979

Without kings and warriors occasional verse fails

Skeletal Kampuchea children staring, cold
Stubborn Irish children throwing grenades
These are objects too serious for verse,
Crushed Soweto children clutching their entrails
Then in verse bruised, mocks

Today no poet sufficiently asks why dying children
Stare or throw bombs. And why should we
Compute painful doubts that will forever occupy us?
Talking oil-crises in our eight-cylinder cars
Is enough travesty...

The year of the child must make no difference then
Where tadpoles are never allowed to grow into frogs!

Notes and Glossary

Notes & Glossary

Bau   A game played, often on a board, by at least two people, one on each side. Thirty-two places are scooped on the board and marbles or stones are placed in the scoops to play. It is popular in East and Central Africa.

Bonongwe   Natural vegetable that is easy to find.

Chambo   An exceptionally delicious fish from Lake Malawi.

Chibuku   Commercial beer, mass-produced (replacing the village brew, *masese*).

Chilembwe   John Chilembwe was the first Malawian rebel missionary to rise against Nyasaland Colonial Government under the banner of Christianity. Oral traditions believe that he did not die at the hands of colonialists but went up to heaven through the *nsolo* tree. See George Simeon Mwase's *Strike A Blow and Die* (African Writers Series 160).

Chingwe's Hole   A hole on Zomba plateau known by this name. It is believed that wrong-doers were dropped into this hole as their punishment. At the bottom of the hole, Namitembo River is believed to originate. Oral testimonies have varied versions of the origins and the uses of the hole, but all agree about its historic significance. 'Glory Be to Chingwe's Hole' has rather obscure reference to a Chewa myth in stanzas two and three. It is the Chewa version of the Greek myth of Pygmalion. Given the current arguments about the role of artists in modern society, the

Chewa version itself is very revealing. Summarizing it here not only clarifies the poem in question but also captures contemporary approaches to the question of artists.

Two men in a village make friends with Frog, a renowned carver. The three always work together on various projects. Every time they go out to cut poles or grass for their houses, they bring home bundles. And each sings to his wife to help him unload his bundle. But Frog sings to his mother as he is not married. The two men always mock Frog for this, after all they are all of marriageable age.

One day when Frog is angered by his friend's mockery he goes into the forest alone and does not return for some time. There he carves a beautiful woman from the heart of a sacred ebony tree. He sticks a pin on the woman's head turning her into a human being. They return home married secretly.

The next time the three friends go out to work they bring home bundles of grass, and Frog sings to his wife to help him carry the grass. The two friends are amused at first but later become so envious at the sight of the beauty of Frog's wife that next day they tell the Chief about it. He sends his army to kill or capture Frog and bring the beauty to him. But Fly overhears the plot and flies to warn Frog of the impending danger.

Frog runs into the forest where he assembles birds, animals, and other creatures and with them plans the rescue of his wife. Dove is chosen to lead the attack by singing a melodious song. Hawk is chosen for his speed and the rest follow Frog. The forest crowd soon gathers at the Chief's palace in a great commotion. The Chief decides to see what the crowd is up to. Suddenly all is quiet. Dove sings his most melodious song. The Chief invites his bride to listen to this lovely music. As they come out of their palace, Hawk, with the speed of lightning, swoops down and picks the pin from the beauty. The Beauty becomes wood again.

Chiuta   God, The Creator, The Almighty, The Most Powerful One, He who creates rainbows (Chiuta literally means Big Bow).

Chopa   The ritual dance of the Lomwe people associated with rain-making, gods, power, fertility etc.

Dondolo   Small, tasteless fish, the easiest to catch.

Kabula   Named after Kabula Hill in Blantyre.

Kachasu   Very strong traditional gin.

Kwangala   Yao word for dancing frantically. The Chief is in the mind of the poet.

Masese   Nutritious beer from maize or millet flour brewed in the villages of Malawi (cf. *chibuku*).

Mphunzi Hills   Known for their rock paintings which attract scholars and tourists (in Dedza District, Central Malawi).

Nakatobwa   A very sweet type of mango found in Mangochi.

Namizimu Mountains   Literally Mountains of Spirits. (Range of mountains bordering Malawi and Moçambique on the eastern bank of the lake.)

Zipini   Nose rings (wooden).

Nsima   Hard porridge made from maize, millet or rice flour.

Nsolo tree   A tree believed to be so strong that it repels lightning (hence Chilembwe's reference).

Shire River   Lake Malawi narrows down at the southern tip into a river called Shire. Shire is pronounced as in She and Re (as in *re*vel).

Thobwa (Tʰobwa)   Sweet brew, usually made from millet.

Zomba   District in Southern Malawi. Once the capital town of Malawi named after the plateau which dominates the town. Several poems in this volume refer to various features of the plateau. The biggest constituent college of the University of Malawi, Chancellor College, as well as the University Central Administration Offices lie at the foot of this plateau.

THE AFRICAN WRITERS SERIES

The book you have been reading is part of Heinemann's long-established series of African fiction. Details of some of the other titles available in this series are given below, but for a catalogue giving information on all the titles available in this series and in the Caribbean Writers Series write to:
Heinemann Educational Publishers
Halley Court, Jordan Hill, Oxford, OX2 8EJ.
United States customers should write to:
Heinemann, 361 Hanover Street,
Portsmouth, NH 03801-3912, USA

JACK MAPANJE
The Chattering Wagtails of Mikuyu Prison

A new collection of poems from Jack Mapanje that both condemns the Malawian regime that incarcerated him and celebrates the love of family and friends and the spirit of his fellow detainees.
Jack Mapanje was released from prison in Malawi at the beginning of May 1991. He had been imprisoned without trial since September 1987. During that time he was a featured Amnesty International Prisoner of Conscience.

SYL CHENEY-COKER
The Blood in The Desert's Eye

'Cheney-Coker strikes me as one of the very few poets in Africa who belong to the international community of letters. Not only does he stand head and shoulders above the others but he refuses to be confined within the denomination "African poet", aiming at something closer to universality . . . Among the most energetic poets writing in Africa.'
Robert Fraser

FRANK CHIPASULA
Whispers in the Wings

'(Frank Chipasula) offers some of the most vivid imagery in all modern African verse.'
Adrian Roscoe, The Quiet Chameleon: Modern Poetry from Central Africa

KOJO LAING
Godhorse

This is a powerful, witty and original collection by Ghana's leading novelist and poet.
Laing's intense yet often playful treatment of themes such as nature, love, death, politics and portraits of daily life ensures that *Godhorse* makes for evocative, ironic and humorous reading.

ADEWALE MAJA-PEARCE (ED)
The Heinemann Book of African Poetry in English

This anthology represents the best African Poetry written in English over the last thirty years. It includes the work of familiar names such as Wole Soyinka, Dennis Brutus and Kojo Laing as well as new talent from the younger generation which includes Chenjerai Hove and Gabriel Gbadamosi.

JACK MAPANJE
Of Chameleons and Gods

'full of fine physical imagery, acute observation and a strong sense of his own roots and values . . . Mapanje is fresh, lively, and inventively aggressive.' *London Magazine*

TANURE OJAIDE
The Blood of Peace

'strong, supple, various, colorful, moving, invariably interesting . . .' *Hayden Carruth, veteran American poet*

'I personally regard him (Ojaide) as perhaps the most important voice in the generation of African writers following Chinua Achebe and Wole Soyinka.'
Joseph Bruchac, The Greenfield Review Literary Center